THE I

6 STEPS FOR LIVING AN EMPOWERED LIFE!

Tamiko Lowry-Pugh

Copyright © 2017 by Tamiko Lowry-Pugh
All rights reserved. No part of this publication may be
reproduced, distributed, or transmitted without the
express consent of the author.

Published By:
Still Standing Publishing Company
Tamiko Lowry-Pugh
www.tamikolowry.com

Printed and bound in the United States of America

ISBN-10: 154125340X:
ISBN-13: 978-1541253407

Contents

Introduction		5
Step 1	THE FEAR FACTOR	9
Step 2	LIVE A LIFE OF PURPOSE	21
Step 3	KNOW YOUR VALUES	33
Step 4	BECOME A GOAL DIGGER	43
Step 5	ULTIMATE SELF-CONFIDENCE	53
Step 6	WALK IN YOUR AUTHENTIC POWER	65
Living The Empowered Life!		77
About the author		79

Tamiko Lowry-Pugh

Introduction

I remember trying to put the pieces of my life back together after going through a marriage that proved to be unhealthy in every sense of the word. I was abused, mentally, verbally, spiritually and at times, even physically.

The divorce papers were signed, and I was off to live my new life as an empowered woman. So I thought. You see, during that marriage, I lost sight of who I was. I was fearful of starting over, I didn't value myself, I didn't understand my life purpose, and my confidence was at an all-time low.

I was now faced with how I felt about myself, my life, and the world around me. After a few years of throwing a pity party, I realized that it was time to put myself first. It was time to be the fearless, purposeful, confident woman that

God called me to be. It was time to take my power back!

In order to rebuild and reclaim your power, you have to start believing in yourself again. You have to start loving yourself again. You have to start walking in your authentic power.

As I went through the journey of rebuilding my life, loving me, and believing in myself, I realized that it wasn't about putting the pieces of my life back together. God was creating something "new" within me, so there were no pieces to put back together. Isaiah 43:19 NKJV says "Behold, I will do a new thing; now shall it spring forth; shall ye not know it? I will even make a way in the wilderness, and rivers in the desert."

The pity party ends now! It's time to be fearless. It's time to discover and live your life purpose. It's time to value yourself. It's time to set goals that move your forward in life. It's time to rebuild your confidence. It's time to walk in your authentic power. It's time to live The Empowered Life!

Tamiko Lowry-Pugh

Step 1

THE FEAR FACTOR

Tamiko Lowry-Pugh

She Believed She Could

So She Did!

The Fear Factor

Did you know that fear is the most common emotion that people are walking around with every day? It is such a common emotion that many people have learned to function with it and never challenge where the fear came from.

Fear is so common that people would rather stay in situations that are destructive and non-productive rather than pursue the blessings that lie beyond the borders of their fears. Fear blinds us to the amazing possibilities of life. Fear limits us and keeps us living in our current situation. But here's the thing… When examined closely we almost always discover that the things and events we fear will simply never happen.

A few years ago I released my first book. I remember the fear that I had when writing it. I feared what people would say about me. I feared that the book wouldn't sell. I feared that my book signing would be empty and no one would show up. I feared what my family would say. I even feared that I wasn't smart enough, and didn't have the platform or expertise to write a book.

When I finally released the book, everything that I feared would happen, did not happen. My book signing was actually filled to capacity, standing room only and I sold out of all the books I had on hand that day. Not only did the book do well with sales, but it became a #1 Amazon Bestseller.

Like I said...FEAR IS NOT REAL!

What does the Bible say about Fear? The Bible gives us a prescription for fear and challenges us to overcome fearful thoughts, behaviors, and attitudes. "The spirit that God gave us does not make us timid, but gives us power, love, and a sound mind." The type of fear that paralyzes us and keeps us from being our best self is simply not the way God wants us to live our lives. We are not designed to live in fear.

Fear is not real!

Did you know that we are only born with 2 fears? We are born with the fear of loud noises, the fear of falling, and possibly the fear of bright lights. That's it! The rest of our fears are learned. We learn them from family and close acquaintances. Our next teacher of fear is us. Our own experiences and our imagination cause us to have fear.

Ask yourself the following questions:

➢ Do your fears intimidate or immobilize you?
➢ Are your fears keeping you from making an

important decision?

➢ Have your fears caused you to be overly concerned with the "what ifs" of life?

If any of these questions ring true for you, the next question is: How long will you allow your fears to control you?

In order to Live The Empowered Life, you MUST face your fears.

Tips for Overcoming Fear

- Acknowledge the fear. Whether it's imagined or real, the first step in overcoming fear is to admit that it exists. We all have fears; it's human nature. Denying or ignoring them doesn't make them go away.
- Analyze it. Where does it come from? Is it real or imagined? Can it be put in a different context? For instance, if you think it through to its logical conclusion, what's the worst that can happen to you? Once you've determined what that might be, ask yourself if you can deal with, or overcome it. More often than not, once you go through the process of analyzing it, the fear isn't as scary as you originally imagined.

- Face it. Allow yourself to feel it, and then do it anyway. Act in spite of your fear and treat is as a challenge for personal growth and an opportunity to become stronger.
- Be persistent. Do the thing you fear over and

over again. By doing it repeatedly, it loses its power over you, and you become less vulnerable to it.

➤ Develop courage. Sometimes the answer may not be to conquer a particular fear; it may be to develop courage. If you focus too much on any one fear instead of trying to build courage, you may end up intesifuing the fear. By developing courage, you begin to build self-confidence and resilience. You also develop a healthy approach towards facing all fear.

Overcoming Fear Exercise

What is your top fear in life? (or around relationships, finance, success, etc.)

_____

Where do you think this fear came from?

_____

Why are you holding on to the fear or how is it serving you?

_____

_____

_____

_____

What would happen if you let go of the fear?

_____

_____

How can you get rid of the fear and when would you be willing to let go of this fear? (List 3 action steps and date.)

_____

_____

_____

_____

_____

Affirmations

I am fearless

I take action now

I am confident and determined

I keep pushing until I succeed

I am willing to release my fears

I trust the process of life

I am divinely protected

I take action without hesitation or fear

I face all my fears head on

I choose faith over fear

Tamiko Lowry-Pugh

Step 2

LIVE A LIFE OF PURPOSE

The purpose of life is to live a life of purpose.

Live a Life of Purpose

It's a common question asked by people all over the world. "What is my purpose in life?" In other words, "Why am I here?" Figuring out your purpose may seem difficult, especially since nowadays, people expect you to have it all figured out at an early age. For a few lucky people, the calling does come early, and they spend their days living out their dreams and life purpose. But what about the rest of us?

In order to become successful and happy in any area of life, you must first create a purpose or mission statement for your life. Personal fulfillment and success come from living the life you were born to live. To live a life of purpose means you're doing what you love to do. You are doing what you're good at, and accomplishing what's important to you. If you really want to be fulfilled, happy, content, and experience inner peace and ultimate fulfillment in life, it's important that you discover your life purpose. Without a purpose as the GPS to guide you, your goals and action plans may not give you the fulfillment that you desire.

I remember wondering what my life purpose was. I would pray to God every day asking him to reveal my life purpose. I thought my life purpose was to rise to the top of the company that I worked for in corporate America with a beautiful office overlooking the city. Even if I didn't enjoy what I was doing. Boy was I wrong! It took me going through several bad relationships and a horrible divorce to discover my life purpose.

You see, I've always been interested in women's empowerment, and working in a field that allowed me to inspire women to be better. But I was in a bad relationship that took away my joy, confidence, fearlessness, and authenticity. I didn't k now who I was anymore, so how could I empower other women when I needed to be empowered?

As I sat in church one Sunday morning, my pastor preached from Romans 8:28. All things work together for the good of them who love the Lord and are called according to His purpose. He went on to say how the things that we go through in life are often connected to our life purpose. At that moment I knew that my purpose of empowering women had to be fulfilled. But not until I was able to overcome and heal from that which disempowered me.

Each and every one of us is born with a unique purpose. We are all here for a reason, and we are all here to serve one another. A life of purpose is not only a true expression of who you really are, but it is your gift to the world. And the world needs what you have to offer. When you are living a life of purpose, you will find greater fulfillment and joy in everything that you do.

Are you currently living a life of purpose? It's time for you to discover your real purpose in life? I'm not talking about your job, your daily responsibilities, or even your long-term goals. I'm talking about the real reason why you were put on this earth. The reason why you exist.

In order to Live The Empowered Life, you MUST live a life of purpose.

Tips to Live a Life of Purpose

1. Live by your beliefs and values
2. Set priorities
3. Follow your passion
4. Achieve balance
5. Feel content
6. Make a difference
7. Live in the moment

Life Purpose Exercise

Write down at least 3 answers to each of the following questions:

What triggers your life dream?

_____

_____

_____

What do you feel driven to do in your life?

_____

_____

_____

What do you love to do?

_____

_____

_____

What do you think you were born to do?

_____

_____

_____

What are you good at?

_____

_____

_____

Compare the answers that are similar and use this to weave together your life purpose mission statement.

Be sure to allow people into your life that support your vision.

Write your life purpose mission statement here:

_____

_____

_____

_____

_____

_____

_____

Affirmations

I am living my life's calling

I am in perfect harmony with purpose

I follow my heart's desire

Joy and contentment fill my life.

I see my life's purpose more clearly

I strive to embrace my true life purpose

I am true to my mission in life

I am creating a life passion and purpose

I live my life with purpose and vision

I have an inspiring mission to fulfill

Step 3

KNOW YOUR VALUES

Open your arms to change,

but don't let go of your values.

— Dalai Lama

Know Your Values

How would you define your values? Before you answer that question, you need to know what, in general, values are. Values are those things that are important to you. Think about what you believe in and what you stand for, and your convictions about what is most important in life. Values are the driving force behind any successful life. Understanding your values will keep your life in balance and help to prioritize goals. Your values mean what and where you place value in life and in what order.

Since these are personal values, you can change values and their order of priority at any time. It's an excellent idea and important exercise to analyze and write down your values at least once a year to see if your life is balanced, and heading in the direction you want it to go. Your priorities will change according to your current values.

If you are trying to accomplish something that is not in alignment with your values, you will never succeed. For instance, if you want more money, but money doesn't rate high as a priority on your list of values, you probably aren't going to become wealthy.

When the things that you do and the way you behave match your values, life is usually good. You're satisfied and content. But when these don't align with your personal values, that's when things feel wrong, which then leads to a real source of unhappiness.

I had a client that came to me because she was unhappy with her thriving business. Although the business was thriving, it was not as successful as she imagined it to be. This was a business that her parents talked her into. She thought that by being a business owner, she would be happy and content. But once I assessed her values, I was able to discover that the type of business she was running was not in alignment with her values and therefore it was not as successful and she was unhappy. This is why making a conscious effort to understand your values is important.

Values exist, whether you recognize them or not. Life can be much easier when you acknowledge your values – and when you make plans and decisions that honor them.

If you value family, but you have to work 70-hour weeks in your job, will you feel internal stress and conflict? And if you don't value competition, and you work in a highly competitive sales environment, are you likely to be satisfied with your job?

In these types of situations, understanding your values can really help. When you know your own values, you can use them to make decisions about how to live your life, and you can answer questions like these:

- ➤ What job should I pursue?
- ➤ Should I accept this promotion?
- ➤ Should I start my own business?
- ➤ Should I compromise, or be firm with my position?
- ➤ Should I follow tradition or travel down a new path?

So, take the time to understand the real priorities in your life, and you'll be able to determine the best direction for you and your life goals.

In order to Live The Empowered Life, you MUST know, understand and honor your values.

Tips for Knowing Your Values

- Values should be somewhat stable, but they don't have strict limits or boundaries. Keep in mind, as you move through life, your values may change. For example, when you start a new career or business, success measured by money and status might be a top priority. But once you have a family, work-life balance may be what you value more.
- As your definition of success changes, so will your personal values. This is why keeping up with your values is a lifelong exercise. You should revisit your values on a regular basis, especially if you start to feel out of balance and can't quite figure out why.
- As you go through the exercise below, keep in mind that values that were important in the past may not be relevant now.

Values Exercise

Identify the times when you were happiest

_____

_____

What were you doing?

_____

_____

Were you with other people? Who?

_____

_____

_____

What other factors contributed to your happiness?

_____

_____

_____

The answers to the previous questions will reveal your current values.

Making value-based choices may not always be easy. However, making a decision that you know is right is a lot less difficult in the long run.

Affirmations

I value myself

I am adding value to the lives of others

I am a person of value

My life is in balance with my core values.

My goals are in agreement with my values

My thoughts support my values

My core values are defined

I live up to my personal beliefs and values

I arrange my life according to my values

I honor my values in all that I do

Step 4

BE A GOAL DIGGER

If the plan doesn't Work,
change the plan but never the goal.

Be a Goal Digger

In order to Live The Empowered Life, you must be a Goal Digger by setting and maintaining crystal clear goals.

It's easy to start off your goal setting routine full of eagerness, enthusiasm, and optimism. But to maintain that drive for the entire year you must set powerful, crystal-clear goals. The first step to getting what you want out of life is to decide exactly what you want.

➢ What do you want to accomplish?
➢ What do you want to experience?
➢ What do you want to achieve? Who do you want to be?

One of the primary reasons most people don't get what they want is that they aren't clear about what they want.

You should set goals in the following areas:

- Financial Goals
- Career/Business Goals
- Free Time/Family Time
- Health/Appearance Goals
- Relationship Goals
- Personal Growth
- Making a Difference

While material goals are fun, your ultimate goal should be to become a master at life.

Have you thought about what you want to be doing in five years from now? Are you clear about what your main objective at work is at the moment? Do you know what you want to have achieved by the end of today?

If you want to succeed, you need to set goals. Without goals, you lack focus and direction. Goal setting not only allows you to take control of your life's direction; it also provides you a benchmark for determining whether you are actually succeeding.

Think about it: Having a million dollars in the bank is only proof of success if one of your goals is to be rich. If your goal is to practice acts of charity, then keeping the money for yourself is suddenly contrary to how you would define success.

To accomplish your goals, you need to know how to set them. You can't just say, "I want" and expect it to happen. Goal setting is a process that starts with careful consideration of what you want to achieve and ends with a lot of hard work to actually do it.

I encourage my clients to set SMART goals. The simple fact is that for goals to be powerful, they should be designed to be SMART.

- Specific.
- Measurable.
- Attainable.
- Relevant.
- Time Bound.

Goal setting is much more than simply saying you want something to happen. Unless you clearly define exactly what you want and understand why you want it the first place, your odds of success are considerably reduced. By following the SMART Goal Setting Formula, you can set goals with confidence and enjoy the satisfaction that comes along with knowing you achieved what you set out to do.

So, what will you decide to accomplish today?

In order to Live The Empowered Life, you MUST be a goal digger.

Goal Setting Tips

- ➢ State each goal as a positive statement
- ➢ Be precise
- ➢ Set priorities
- ➢ Write goals
- ➢ Keep operational goals small
- ➢ Set performance goals, not outcome goals
- ➢ Set realistic goals

It's important to remember that failing to meet goals is not a big deal, just as long as you learn from the experience.

Goal Setting Exercise

Answer the following questions thoroughly:

What do you want to achieve in your life at this time?

_____

_____

_____

Why do you want it? (The mission behind the goal)

_____

_____

_____

When do you want to accomplish it? (Give a date)

___

How will you know when you get it? (What will it look like or feel like. Emotions)

___

___

___

How do you think you can get it? (Action steps) Create 3-5 action steps with a date for each one.

___

___

Affirmations

I review my goals daily

I visualize the achievement of my goals

I'm on the path of success

I accomplish everything I set out to do

I plan my work, and I work my plan

I have the power to achieve any goal

I easily reach my goals on time

All my goals are in perfect harmony

I believe in my goals

I achieve my goals

Step 5

ULTIMATE SELF-CONFIDENCE

The best accessory a girl can own is confidence.

Ultimate Self-Confidence

From the quietly confident doctor whose advice we rely on, to the charismatic confidence of an inspiring speaker, self-confident people have qualities that everyone admires.

When I first started my career as a life coach and speaker, I was very insecure about my abilities to deliver. My mentor at the time, a co-pastor, author and world renowned sought after speaker, gave me the most profound, yet simple advice that changed the way I would view myself forever. She told me:

"If you don't think very highly of yourself, you can't expect anyone else to think it of you."

Basically, what she was saying was that we

alone are responsible for building up our self-confidence.

You can't depend on or wait for anyone else's approval. You have to see yourself as worthy and capable of achieving anything you set your mind on and choose to achieve.

Ultimately, how you see yourself is more important than how anyone else sees you. If you do not work on loving and accepting yourself, nothing anyone else thinks will matter.

Self-confidence is vital in almost every aspect of your life, yet so many people struggle to find it. Sadly, this can be a vicious circle: When you lack self-confidence, you find it difficult to become successful.

After all, most people are reluctant to back a project that's being pitched by someone who was nervous, fumbling, and overly apologetic.

On the other hand, you might be persuaded by someone who speaks clearly, who holds their head up high, who can answer questions with assurance, and who readily admits when he or she does not know something.

Confident people inspire confidence in other people. Their audience, peers, bosses, their customers, and their friends. Gaining the confidence of others is one of the key ways in which a confident person finds success.

The good news is that self-confidence really can be learned and built on. And, whether you're working on your own confidence or building the confidence of people around you, it's well-worth the effort!

Self-confidence is all about balance. At one extreme, we have people with low confidence.

At the other end, we have people who may be over-confident.

Always keep yourself grounded. If not, you will become over-confident and maybe even a bit cocky. Remember, there is a difference between being confidence and being cocky.

Two main things contribute to self-confidence: Self-efficacy (the capacity for producing a desired result) and self-esteem.

You can develop it with these three steps:

- ➢ Prepare for your journey.
- ➢ Set out on your journey.
- ➢ Accelerate towards success.

AFFIRMATION:
I HAVE THE LIGHT OF
GOD INSIDE OF ME.
AS I FOCUS ON MY
INNER GLOW, I AM
FILLED WITH LOVE.

Tamika Lowry Pugh
The Empowering Diva™

Goal setting is probably the most important activity that you can learn in order to improve your self-confidence. (Refer to step 4)

In order to Live The Empowered Life, you MUST have ultimate self-confidence.

Tips for Building Ultimate Self-Confidence

- ➢ Acknowledge Your Uniqueness. Believe in yourself and know that you are one of a kind.
- ➢ Give it Your Best. When you do the best you can, with the best of what you have, you can't help but feel good about yourself.
- ➢ Persevere. Everyone has setbacks and obstacles to deal with. Don't let them undermine your confidence.
- ➢ Overcome adversity. Overcoming adversity will build and strengthen your self-confidence.
- ➢ Accomplish something. Set goals for yourself and then push yourself to reach them. Self-confidence soars when you know you can do what you put your mind to.
- ➢ Separate Yourself From the Event. You are not defined by what happens to you, nor are you defined by how others see you.
- ➢ Confront your fears. There is nothing that can

destroy self-confidence more than succumbing to fear.
- Good looks do not equal self-confidence. Some of the most attractive people in the world are insecure and lack self-confidence.
- Take good care of yourself. When you are fit, in good health, and make a point of looking your best, you can't help but feel confident.
- Learn how to give yourself a pep talk. We all have our down moments, moments of doubt, confusion and uncertainty. When that happens, we must learn how to restore self-confidence.

Self-confidence is vital to achieving success in any area of life. You acquire it by doing, learning, accomplishing, and persisting.

Self-Confidence Exercise

Become aware. Know who you are and what you want. As the saying goes "If you don't know where you are going, how will you know when you get there?" Use the following chart or a separate excel spreadsheet to outline your strengths, what you enjoy doing, and how you can establish goals. List the things you'd like to do and what you have to do to accomplish them.

Strengths	Personal Abilities	Physical Abilities	Interests

To accomplish my self-confidence goals I will:

_____

_____

_____

_____

_____

_____

_____

_____

_____

Affirmations

I approve of myself

I love myself deeply and completely

I am confident of the future

I am bold and outgoing

I am energetic and enthusiastic

I am self-reliant, creative and persistent

I am confident

I am strong and powerful

I believe in myself

I confidently meet any challenge

Step 6

WALK IN YOUR AUTHENTIC POWER

Be who you were created to be, and you will set the world on fire.

Walk in Your Authentic Power

In order to Live The Empowered Life you have to explore and connect to your authentic self and align your life with who you really are! When you walk in your authentic power, you can begin living life according to your own needs and values rather than those that society, friends, and family expect from you.

To walk in your authentic power, you have to stop comparing yourself to other people. Point Blank! No one in the entire world can do a better job at being you than you! Don't be afraid to be different, to be unique, and to be original.

It takes It takes courage and self-confidence to walk in your authentic power. To reveal your uniqueness and to show that you are one of a kind.

As the late Steve Jobs noted in his speech at a Stanford University graduation commencement:
"Your time is limited; so don't waste it living someone else's life. Don't be trapped by dogma - which is living with the results of other people's thinking. Don't let the noise of others' opinions drown out your own inner voice. And most important, have the courage to follow your heart and intuition. They somehow already know what you truly want to become. Everything else is secondary."

It's true. Life is too short to live it trying to be anything other than your true, authentic self. Be who you are, and be it the best way you know how. Celebrate your individuality and uniqueness.

Walk in your authentic power!

Know who you are. Before you can be yourself, you must know who that is, and then be true to that self. Many centuries ago Socrates wisely observed that self-knowledge is the pillar of all virtue. Without it nothing else is genuine.

Trust your intuition and instincts. Part of knowing who you are and being authentic is trusting your intuition and instincts. We all have an inner gauge that guides us along our most fulfilling path. Look deep within to find the answers to your life. No one is better at knowing what you need and want from life than you. Of course, it is important to listen to the advice of family, friends, and professionals, but you are the ultimate authority on you. You are unique and original, and no one but you can make your decisions for you. To go against that intuition is to go against your fundamental nature and source of satisfaction.

Express yourself by cultivating your own style, tastes and personality. Many people try to be like those who seem to be popular. Rather than work on developing themselves they try to copy others and lose themselves in the process. Much time is wasted in such pursuits, and the results are disillusionment and feelings of failure. When you work on cultivating your own style, tastes and personality, not only are you genuine and authentic, you're more interesting and attractive to others. Let go of fear and embrace your authenticity. Make your life an expression of who you are.

As Steve Jobs said, have the courage to follow your heart. If you desire to be an artist, don't settle for being an accountant because your parents want you to be, or because you can make more money at it. In the end, you will lose out because the money won't matter if you're unhappy, unmotivated or depressed.

Believe in yourself and don't worry about what other people think. When you choose the right path for yourself, do not allow the opinions of others to distract you. People are good at offering well-intentioned, unsolicited opinions, however only you know what's best for you. Don't let a lack of self-confidence or self-doubt prevent you from pursuing what you know is best for you. Begin to let go of your personal insecurities. If you strive to be someone you're not, you will never be happy. Be yourself. Be proud of who you are.

Walk in your authentic power!

When you walk in your authentic power, you are showing the world that you are confident, courageous, strong, and vibrant.

In order to Live The Empowered Life, you MUST walk in your authentic power.

Tips for Walking in Your Authentic Power

- Be who you are, be your genuine self
- Follow your own value system
- Listen to the advice of others, but make up your own mind
- Recognize, appreciate, and develop your unique talents
- Stand up for what you believe in, and you will gain respect
- Know that being 'different' is a gift
- Understand that you are enriching others by being yourself

Authentic Power Exercise

If you are ready to walk in your authentic power, ask yourself these 5 questions:

1. When you were little, what did you want to be when you grew up? (You can still be that)

_____

_____

_____

2. What makes you laugh? (Give yourself permission to laugh out loud)

_____

_____

3. What clothes do you feel comfortable in? (Clothes are a way of expressing yourself and what you wear should be comfortable and should reflect the true you).

_____

_____

4. What activities do you enjoy? Discovering these activities will help guide you towards a place where you want to spend time.

_____

_____

_____

5. Who can you be yourself around? We are social creatures by nature, so it is important to spend time with people who make us feel good and accept us for who we really are. (spend more time with those people)

Affirmations

When I am my true self, I feel at ease

My fun-loving side helps others warm up to me

I share my opinions freely

I commit to being myself

I love myself, and I accept myself as I am

I stand up for what you believe in

I appreciate my unique talents

I am interesting and attractive to others

I am true to myself

I am walking in my authentic power

Living The Empowered Life!

There you have it! The Empowerment Formula: 6 Steps For Living An Empowered Life! This formula was created to equip you to live an empowered life of passion, purpose, potential, and peace so that you can become the empowered woman you were created to be.

I encourage you to implement one step at a time until you have mastered each one of them. Keep in mind that that Living The Empowered Life is not a one shot deal. It's an ongoing process, that takes haed work, commitment, persistence, and action.

Once you implement The Empowerment Formula, you will begin to live your best life, full of passion while embracing your purpose and maximizing the full potential that God has placed inside of you.

You see, the purpose of life is to grow and to become all that you were intended to be. Ignite your passion, embrace your purpose, maximize your potential, and be at peace.

Here's to Living The Empowered Life!

About The Author

Tamiko Lowry-Pugh often referred to as "The Empowering Diva" is the voice for Women's Empowerment. As the CEO of EmpowerME! Life Coaching & Consulting, and The founder of The Still Standing Foundation, she has constructed a powerful movement dedicated to the empowerment and personal development of women across the world.

As an International Bestselling Author, Inspirational Speaker, Empowerment Specialist, and Domestic Violence Educator, Tamiko believes that empowerment comes from within and can be achieved by honoring yourself, your values, and expressing your talents and gifts.
www.tamikolowry.com

Made in the USA
Lexington, KY
03 March 2018